Vocal Score

WEST SIDE STORY®

Based on a conception of Jerome Robbins

Book by
Arthur Laurents

Music by
Leonard Bernstein®

Lyrics by
Stephen Sondheim

Entire original production
directed and choreographed by
Jerome Robbins

ISBN 0-634-04678-0

LEONARD
BERNSTEIN
*Music Publishing
Company LLC*

BOOSEY & HAWKES

HAL•LEONARD®
CORPORATION
7777 W. BLUEMOUND RD. P.O. BOX 13819 MILWAUKEE, WI 53213

Visit Hal Leonard Online at
www.halleonard.com

Facsimile from the composer's manuscript of *Cool*

CONTENTS

Act I

Scene 1   **The neighborhood**

Scene 2   **A back yard**

Scene 3   **The bridal shop**

Scene 4   **The gym**

The Dance at the Gym:

Scene 5   **A back alley**

Scene 6   **The drugstore**

Scene 7   **The bridal shop**

Scene 8   **The neighborhood**

Scene 9   **Under the highway**

Act II

Appendices

ABOUT *WEST SIDE STORY*

In 1985, the authors of West Side Story *came together at a Dramatists Guild Landmark Symposium to discuss their work. Terrence McNally acted as Moderator. The transcript of the entire session was published in the Dramatists Guild Quarterly (Autumn 1985). In the following excerpts, Jerome Robbins and Leonard Bernstein discuss the origin of the show and the collaboration that produced it.*

TERRENCE McNALLY: It's hard to imagine what the musical theater would be like in 1985 without the efforts of the four gentlemen sitting here with me, the authors of *West Side Story*. In our theater community, they are held in great, great respect and much love. *West Side Story* is the one time these four extraordinary talents came together. I'd like to start with the germ of the idea, the first time somebody said, "Hey, there's a musical there," up through opening night in New York, in this case September 26, 1957, when *West Side Story* opened at the Winter Garden Theater.

JEROME ROBBINS: I don't remember the exact date – it was somewhere around 1949 – a friend of mine was offered the role of Romeo. He said to me, "This part seems very passive, would you tell me what you think I should do with it." I tried to imagine it in terms of today. That clicked in, and I said to myself, "There's a wonderful idea here." So I wrote a very brief outline and started looking for a producer and collaborators who'd be interested. This was not easy. Producers were not at all interested in doing it. Arthur and Lenny were interested, but not in getting together to work on it at that time, so we put it away. Many years later, they were involved in another musical and asked me to join them. I was not interested in *their* musical, but I did manage to say, "How about *Romeo and Juliet?*" I won them back to the subject, and that started our collaboration.

McNALLY: Were Arthur and Lenny the first librettist and composer you approached?

ROBBINS: Oh, yes. During the long period we put the project aside, I wasn't actively seeking other collaborators, I thought these were the best people for the material. I stuck to trying to get these guys, and when they came back to me I had the bait to grab them. …

McNALLY: Lenny, part of the *West Side Story* lore is that you intended to do the lyrics yourself. Is that true?

LEONARD BERNSTEIN: …Yes, when we began I had – madly – undertaken to do the lyrics as well as the music. In 1955, I was also working on another show, *Candide*, and then the *West Side Story* music turned out to be extraordinarily balletic – which I was very happy about – and turned out to be a tremendously greater amount of music than I had expected, ballet music, symphonic music, developmental music. For those two reasons, I realized that I couldn't do all that music, plus the lyrics, and do them well. Arthur mentioned that he'd heard a young fellow named Stephen Sondheim sing some of his songs at a party. … I freaked out when Steve came in and sang his songs. From that moment to this, we've been loving colleagues and friends. …

ROBBINS: I'd like to talk a little bit about that period, because it was one of the most exciting I've ever had in the theater: the period of the collaboration, when we were feeding each other all the time. We would meet wherever we could, depending on our schedules. Arthur would come in with a scene, the others would say they could do a song on this material, I'd supply, "How about if we did this as a dance?" There was this wonderful, mutual exchange going on. We can talk here about details, "I did this, I did that," but the essence of it was what we gave to each other, took from each other, yielded to each other, surrendered, reworked, put back together again, all of those things. It was a very important and extraordinary time. The collaboration was most fruitful during that digestive period. I say that because we got turned down so much, and for so many reasons, that we kept going back to the script, or rather our play, saying, "That didn't work, I wonder why not, what didn't they like, let's take a look at it again."

I remember Richard Rodger's contribution. We had a death scene for Maria — she was going to commit suicide or something, as in Shakespeare. He said, "She's dead already, after this all happens to her." So the walls we hit were helpful to us in a way, sending us back for another look. I'm glad we didn't get *West Side Story* on right away. Between the time we thought of it and finally did it, we did an immense amount of work on it.

BERNSTEIN: Amen to that. This was one of the most extraordinary collaborations of my life, perhaps *the* most, in that very sense of our nourishing one another. There was a generosity on everybody's part that I've rarely seen in the theater. For example, the song "Something's Coming" was a very late comer. We realized we needed a character-introduction kind of song for Tony. There was a marvelous introductory page in the script that Arthur had written, a kind of monologue, the essence of which became the lyric for this song. We raped Arthur's playwriting. I've never seen anyone so encouraging, let alone generous, urging us, "Yes, take it, take it, make it a song."

Reprinted from *The Dramatists Guild Quarterly* © 1985. All rights reserved.
With thanks to Terrence McNally and the Estate of Jerome Robbins.

VORWORT ZU WEST SIDE STORY

Die Urheber von West Side Story kamen 1985 bei einem Dramatists Guild Landmark Symposium zusammen, um über ihr Werk zu sprechen. Terrence McNally war als Moderator dabei. Diese Gespräche wurden vollständig in der Herbstausgabe 1985 des Dramatists Guild Quarterly veröffentlicht. An dieser Stelle bringen wir auszugsweise Erinnerungen von Jerome Robbins und Leonard Bernstein an die Anfänge dieser Show und die Zusammenarbeit, die schließlich zu ihrer Produktion führte.

TERRENCE MCNALLY: Man kann sich die Situation im Musiktheater 1985 ohne die vier Urheber von *West Side Story*, mit denen ich hier zusammensitze, kaum vorstellen. Unter Theaterleuten empfindet man großen Respekt und ein Gefühl der Liebe für sie. In *West Side Story* sind vier Talente auf eine einmalige Weise zusammengekommen. Ich möchte diese Diskussion mit der anfänglichen Idee beginnen, d. h. mit dem Zeitpunkt, zu dem jemand sagte, "Daraus läßt sich ein Musical machen!" und dann weitergehen bis zur Premiere in New York, die am 26. September 1957 stattfand, als Theaterbesuchern *West Side Story* erstmalig im Winter Garden Theater geboten wurde.

JEROME ROBBINS: An das genaue Datum kann ich mich nicht erinnern - aber es war um 1949 - als einem Freund von mir die Romeo-Rolle angeboten wurde. Er sagte zu mir, "Diese Rolle scheint sehr passiv zu sein; kannst du mir sagen, was ich damit anfangen soll?" Ich versuchte, Romeo in heutigen Zusammenhängen zu sehen. Da ist dann der Groschen gefallen, und ich sagte mir, "die Grundidee ist ganz wunderbar!" Also schrieb ich einen skizzenhaften Umriß und sah mich nach einem Produzenten und interessierten Mitarbeitern um. Das war gar nicht so einfach. Die meisten Produzenten hatten überhaupt kein Interesse an der Geschichte. Arthur und Lenny waren zwar interessiert, doch nicht ausreichend, um sich zusammenzusetzen und daran zu arbeiten; so wurde die Idee auf ein totes Gleis geschoben. Erst viele Jahre später, als die Beiden an einem anderen Musical arbeiteten, forderten sie mich auf, mitzumachen. Ich war zwar an ihrem Stück nicht interessiert, doch sagte ich, "Wie wär's mit Romeo und Julia?" Ich konnte sie für diesen Stoff zurückgewinnen, und so fing unsere Zusammenarbeit an.

MCNALLY: Waren Arthur und Lenny der erste Librettist und Komponist, denen Sie mit dieser Idee kamen?

ROBBINS: O ja! Während der ganzen Zeit, als das Projekt unbeachtet blieb, habe ich mich nicht aktiv nach anderen Mitarbeitern umgesehen. Ich hielt diese beiden noch immer für die besten dafür. Ich blieb dabei, daß ich sie haben wollte, und als sie zu mir zurückkamen, hatte ich genau den richtigen Köder für sie ....."

MCNALLY: Lenny, eine der *West Side Story*-Legenden ist, daß Sie den Text selber schreiben wollten. Stimmt das?

LEONARD BERNSTEIN: ..... Ja, als wir anfingen, hatte ich die - zugegeben verrückte - Absicht, sowohl den Text als auch die Musik selbst zu schreiben. Doch arbeitete ich 1955 bereits an "Candide", und es stellte sich heraus, daß die Musik für *West Side Story* überaus ballettartig war - worüber ich sehr froh war - und daß es sich um viel mehr Musik handelte, als ich erwartet hatte - Ballettmusik, symphonische Musik, Entwicklungsmusik. Aus diesen Gründen erkannte ich, daß ich nicht alles - die Musik und den Text - allein schaffen konnte. Dann erwähnte Arthur, daß ein junger Mann, Stephen Sondheim, einige seiner Songs auf einer Party gesungen hatte ..... Mir wurde ganz anders, als Steve kam und seine Songs zum besten gab. Von dem Moment an wurden wir Kollegen und Freunde und sind es bis heute geblieben .....

ROBBINS: Darüber möchte ich mich noch weiter unterhalten, denn es war die aufregendste Zeit meines Theaterlebens: diese Zeit der Zusammenarbeit, als wir uns gegenseitig dauernd schöpferische Bissen zuschoben. Wir sind zusammengekommen, sooft wir konnten, je nach unseren eigenen Arbeitsplänen. Da konnte es sein, daß Arthur eine der Szenen mitbrachte und die anderen sagten, sie könnten dafür die Musik schreiben. Ich mag gesagt haben, "Wie wäre das als ein Tanz?" Wir hatten diesen wunderbaren geistigen Austausch damals. Jetzt können wir über Einzelheiten reden und sagen "dies und jenes habe ich gemacht," aber damals war das Wesentliche, was wir einander gegeben und voneinander genommen haben, wo wir nachgegeben, umgearbeitet und das Ganze wieder zusammengebaut haben, all das. Es war eine sehr wichtige und ungewöhnliche Zeit. Unsere Zusammenarbeit war während dieser Verdauungsperiode am fruchtbarsten. Ich sage immer wieder, daß wir deshalb auf den Text, oder vielmehr unser Stück, zurückgekommen sind, weil wir so viele Ablehnungen aus so vielen verschiedenen Gründen erfahren haben, und wir uns sagten, " So ging es also nicht, die Frage ist, warum nicht; was hat ihnen nicht gefallen? Also müssen wir das anders machen."

Ich kann mich noch gut an Richard Rodgers erinnern. Wir arbeiteten an der Sterbeszene für Maria - sie sollte Selbstmord begehen oder so ähnlich, wie bei Shakespeare. Er sagte, "nach all dem, was ihr geschehen ist, ist sie schon so gut wie tot." In dem Fall waren also die Wände, gegen die wir gerannt sind, gut für uns, denn wir mußten wieder zurück und unsere Arbeit noch einmal betrachten. Ich bin froh, daß wir West Side Story nicht gleich richtig hingekriegt haben. Von dem Moment an, wo wir nur über dieses Stück nachgedacht haben, bis es endlich fertig war, haben wir unheimlich viel Arbeit geleistet.

BERNSTEIN: Dazu kann ich nur "Ja und Amen" sagen. Es war eine der erstaunlichsten Perioden der Zusammenarbeiten in meinem Leben, vielleicht sogar die erstaunlichste, wenn man diese gegenseitige Befruchtung bedenkt. Alle, die daran arbeiteten, zeigten eine Großzügigkeit, die ich sonst in der Theaterwelt kaum gesehen habe. Zum Beispiel kam das Lied "Something's Coming" ziemlich spät zustande. Wir wußten, daß wir für Tonys Einführung ein Lied brauchten. Der Text, den Arthur geschrieben hatte, enthielt eine wunderbare Seite, eine Art Monolog, dessen Essenz in diesem Lied ausgedrückt wurde. Wir haben Arthurs Text schamlos ausgeraubt. Ich habe nie zuvor jemanden gekannt, der so ermutigend, so großmütig war, und uns anfeuerte, "Ja, nehmt es, nehmt es und macht ein Lied daraus".

Nachdruck aus *The Dramatists Guild Quarterly* © 1985. Alle Rechte vorbehalten.
Wir danken Terrence McNally und der Hinterlassenschaft von Jerome Robbins.

A PROPOS DE WEST SIDE STORY

En 1985, les auteurs de West Side Story se réunirent lors d'un symposium de la Dramatists Guild sur les œuvres ayant fait date pour discuter de leur œuvre, avec Terrence McNally comme modérateur. La transcription de toute cette session a été publiée dans le numéro d'automne 1985 du Dramatists Guild Quarterly (Bulletin trimestriel de la confrérie des dramaturges). Dans les extraits ci-après, Jerome Robbins et Leonard Bernstein s'entretiennent sur l'origine de ce spectacle et la collaboration qui a permis de la réaliser.

TERRENCE McNALLY : On a du mal à imaginer ce qu'aurait été la comédie musicale en 1985 sans les efforts des quatre auteurs de *West Side Story,* assis ici avec moi. Dans le milieu du théâtre, ils inspirent énormément de respect et d'affection. *West Side Story,* c'est la seule fois où ces quatre talents extraordinaires ont collaboré. J'aimerais commencer avec le germe de l'idée, la première fois qu'on a dit : « Voilà un beau sujet de comédie musicale, » et continuer jusqu'à la première à New York, le 26 septembre 1957, lorsque *West Side Story* a débuté au Winter Garden Theater.

JEROME ROBBINS : Je ne me souviens pas de la date exacte, ça devait être aux environs de 1949, où on a offert à un de mes copains le rôle de Roméo. Il me demanda : « Ce rôle me paraît bien passif. A ton avis, qu'est ce que je pourrais bien en faire. » J'essayai de me l'imaginer dans un contexte moderne. Ça a fait tilt et je me suis dit « Il y a une idée formidable là dedans. » J'écrivis donc un court synopsis et commençai à chercher un producteur et des collaborateurs que ça risquerait d'intéresser. Ça n'a pas été facile. Les producteurs ne voulaient rien avoir affaire avec. Arthur et Lenny étaient intéressés mais pas pour y travailler ensemble à ce moment-là. On l'a donc mis de côté. Des années plus tard, alors qu'ils collaboraient à une autre comédie musicale ils me demandèrent de me joindre à eux. Je n'étais pas intéressé par *leur* comédie musicale, mais m'arrangeai quand même pour leur dire : « Et Roméo et Juliette ? » J'arrivai à leur faire accepter le sujet et ça a été le début de notre collaboration.

McNALLY : Est-ce que Arthur et Lenny furent les premiers librettiste et compositeur que vous ayez contactés ?

ROBBINS : Bien sûr. Pendant toute la longue période où ce projet avait été mis de côté je n'avais pas vraiment cherché d'autres collaborateurs car je pensais qu'ils étaient les meilleurs pour ce sujet. J'ai toujours essayé d'avoir ces gars-là et quand ils sont revenus dans mon camp, j'avais ce qu'il fallait pour les accrocher...

McNALLY : Lenny, on raconte que vous aviez l'intention d'écrire vous-même les paroles de *West Side Story.* C'est vrai ?

LEONARD BERNSTEIN : ...Oui, quand nous avons commencé, j'avais décidé de façon dingue d'écrire aussi bien les paroles que la musique. En 1955, je travaillais également à une autre comédie musicale, *Candide,* et puis, la musique de *West Side Story* s'avéra être terriblement axée sur la danse, ce dont j'étais très heureux, et nécessiter beaucoup plus de musique que je ne l'avais escompté : musique de ballet, musique symphonique, développement musical. Pour ces deux raisons, je me rendis compte que je ne pouvais pas écrire à la fois toute cette musique plus les paroles et tout faire bien. Arthur mentionna qu'il avait entendu un jeune gars nommé Stephen Sondheim chanter quelques unes de ses chansons à une réception... Je n'en suis pas revenu lorsque Steve est venu chanter ses chansons. C'est depuis ce temps là, et jusqu'à maintenant, que nous sommes des collègues et des amis très cordiaux...

ROBBINS : J'aimerais parler un peu de cette période, car c'est l'une des plus passionnantes que j'aie jamais connu au théâtre : la période de la collaboration, lorsque nous nous encouragions mutuellement sans arrêt. On se réunissait où on pouvait, selon notre emploi du temps. Arthur arrivait avec une scène, les autres disaient qu'ils pouvaient écrire une chanson sur le texte et moi je proposais : « Pourquoi pas faire ça sous forme de danse ? » Il y avait un échange formidable entre nous. On pourrait parler ici de détails : « J'ai fait ceci, j'ai fait cela, » mais en réalité c'est ce que nous nous sommes donné les uns aux autres, ce que nous avons pris les uns aux autres, cédé les uns aux autres, abandonné, remanié, remis ensemble, c'est tout ça. Ça a vraiment été une époque importante et formidable. Notre collaboration a été très fructueuse durant la période de gestation. Je dis ça car on nous a refusé des tas de choses et pour tellement de raisons, que nous retournions constamment au script, ou plutôt à la pièce en disant : « Ça n'a pas marché, je me demande bien pourquoi, qu'est-ce qu'ils n'ont pas aimé, revoyons donc tout ça. »

Je me souviens de ce qu'a contribué Richard Rodgers. Nous avions une scène où Maria devait mourir, elle allait se suicider ou quelque chose comme ça, comme dans Shakespeare. Il nous dit : « Elle est déjà morte après tout ce qui lui arrive. » Dans une certaine mesure, de nous être heurté à un mur nous a servi, puisque cela nous a obligé à tout revoir. Je suis content que *West Side Story* n'ait pas marché immédiatement. Entre le moment où nous y avons pensé et celui où nous l'avons finalement réalisé, nous y avons consacré un travail considérable.

BERNSTEIN : Tout à fait d'accord. Il s'agit-là d'une des plus extraordinaires collaborations de ma vie, peut être même la plus extraordinaire en ce sens que nous nous encouragions mutuellement. Tout le monde faisait preuve d'une générosité que j'ai rarement vue au théâtre. Par exemple, la chanson « Something's Coming » n'a été écrite que très tard. Nous savions que nous avions besoin pour Tony d'une chanson servant à présenter ce personnage. Il y avait une merveilleuse page d'introduction dans le script qu'Arthur avait écrit, un genre de monologue, qui inspira les paroles de cette chanson. Nous avons pillé la pièce d'Arthur. Je n'ai jamais vu quelqu'un d'aussi encourageant, sans parler de généreux. Il nous poussait en disant : « Bien sûr, prenez-la, prenez-la, faites-en une chanson. »

Tiré du *The Dramatist Guild Quarterly* © 1985. Tous droits réservés.
Avec nos remerciements à Terrence McNally et à la succession de Jerome Robbins.

Editors' Note

When Leonard Bernstein conducted *West Side Story* for the Deutsche Grammophon recording sessions in 1984, he took the opportunity to look at the score not only as the conductor but also as the composer. He made several revisions, specifying that these should appear in the publication of the score. Preparation of the full score was immediately begun, but was interrupted by Mr. Bernstein's death in 1990. The full score was printed by Boosey & Hawkes in 1994, and all of Mr. Bernstein's revisions were incorporated into that publication.

Now the time has come for the publication of a piano/vocal score to match. We've taken this opportunity to revise several elements in this score. For one, there is now a bar count, with bar numbers in rehearsal boxes matching those in the full score. The names of the characters now appear in the left margin, next to the music those characters sing. There are instrumental cues throughout, so that this piano/vocal may be truly considered a piano/conductor score as well. The preliminary pages have been expanded to include the instrumentation, licensing information, the duration of the work, and information about the Deutsche Grammophon recording.

Even though Mr. Bernstein made his wishes very clear regarding the "Overture", in that it should not appear at the start of the full score, we have included a piano reduction of it here, as an appendix. A second appendix includes information about the cast and credits of the film of *West Side Story*. Please note that this revised piano/vocal score does not include any of the musical alterations from the film; this score presents the work as the staged theater piece originally intended by the authors.

Musically, this revised piano/vocal reflects much more accurately what actually happens in the orchestration. For instance, in the original piano/vocal, the left hand in bars 72-79 of the "Mambo" played on the offbeats and made plenty of noise, but it wasn't at all what the orchestra plays. This passage has been altered now to be both accurate and pianistic. At the beginning of the "Quintet" the right hand now plays different octaves, in accordance to the octaves played by sections of the orchestra. In another instance, the beginning of Number 13 (the ballet in the second act) was written on three staves; this passage is easier to read on two staves in the revised score, and all the notes are still there.

In every instance, the music appears more accessible now. The vocal lines are easier to read with beams over groups of notes of less than a quarter value. In the piano reduction, the fiendishly difficult dance music is still difficult, but now there are cue-size notes indicating what may be left out, if the music is beyond your keyboard technique. Many passages are now more easily spread between the two hands.

We would like to thank Tom Hooper for his expert assistance in entering into computer files much of this new edition. Thanks also to Holly Mentzer, of Boosey & Hawkes, Inc., and to Rick Sanford.

We feel certain that this revised score would have been welcomed by Mr. Bernstein, and we hope that it will serve his music well for many years to come.

Seann Alderking and Charlie Harmon
1999

Anmerkung des Herausgebers

Als Leonard Bernstein *West Side Story* 1984 für die Tonaufnahme der Deutschen Grammophon dirigierte, nahm er die Gelegenheit wahr, die Partitur nicht nur aus der Sicht des Dirigenten, sondern auch als Komponist zu sehen. Er machte einige Änderungen mit der Anweisung, daß diese in der veröffentlichten Partitur erscheinen sollten. Die Vorbereitungen für die komplette Partitur wurden sofort in die Wege geleitet, jedoch wurden sie 1990 durch Leonard Bernsteins Tod unterbrochen. Die komplette Partitur wurde von Boosey & Hawkes 1994 herausgegeben, und enthielt alle Änderungen, die Bernstein vorgenommen hatte.

Jetzt ist der Zeitpunkt für die Herausgabe einer Klavierauszug gekommen. Dabei haben wir einige Elemente der früheren Partitur revidiert. Zum Beispiel wurden die Takte numeriert, wobei die Zahlen im Probenabschnitt mit denen der kompletten Partitur übereinstimmen. In dieser Ausgabe stehen die Namen der handelnden Personen links im Rand neben der Musik, die sie singen. Markierungen für die Instrumente erscheinen durchweg, so daß diese Klavierauszug wirklich als Klavier-/Dirigentenpartitur betrachtet werden kann. Die ersten Seiten wurden mit Notizen zur Instrumentation, Lizenzinformation, der Dauer der Aufführung und Angaben über die Aufnahme der Deutschen Grammophon erweitert.

Zwar kannten wir Leonard Bernsteins Wünsche in bezug auf die "Overtüre", d.h. er wollte nicht, daß sie am Anfang der kompletten Partitur stehen sollte, doch haben wir eine verkürzte Version für Klavier als Anhang eingeschoben. Ein zweiter Anhang enthält Informationen über die Darsteller und Quellenangaben für den Film *West Side Story*. Es ist zu beachten, daß diese überarbeitete Klavierauszug keine der musikalischen Änderungen enthält, die für den Film vorgenommen wurden; diese Partitur bringt das Werk als ein Bühnenstück, wie es von den Autoren ursprünglich vorgesehen war.

In musikalischer Hinsicht hält sich diese überarbeitete Klavierauszug getreuer an die Orchestration. Zum Beispiel spielte die linke Hand in der Original-Partitur in den Takten 72-79 des "Mambo" die Auftakte und zwar ziemlich laut; doch war das nicht die Musik, die das Orchester spielt. Diese Stelle wurde jetzt dahin geändert, daß sie mit dem Orchester genauer übereinstimmt und auf dem Klavier gespielt werden kann. Hier spielt die rechte Hand am Anfang des "Quintetts" in Anlehnung an das Orchester andere Oktaven. An einer anderen Stelle in der früheren Fassung wurde der Anfang von Nummer 13 (das Ballett im zweiten Akt) über drei Notenlinien hin geschrieben; diese Stelle ist in der überarbeiteten Partitur über zwei Linien hin einfacher zu lesen, doch sind alle Noten da.

Die Musik wurde in jeder Hinsicht besser zugänglich gemacht. Die Singstimmen sind einfacher zu lesen, da oberhalb der Notengruppen unter einem Viertelwert ein Bogen gesetzt wurde. In der Klavierversion ist die äußerst schwierige Tanzmusik immer noch schwierig, doch wurden die Stellen markiert, die ausgelassen werden können, wenn die Klavierkunst für die Musik nicht ausreicht. An vielen Stellen besteht eine bessere Balance zwischen beiden Händen.

Wir möchten Tom Hooper für seine sachkundige Hilfe unseren Dank aussprechen; er hat einen großen Teil dieser Ausgabe in Computerdateien eingegeben. Auch danken wir Holly Mentzer von Boosey & Hawkes, Inc., und Rick Sanford.

Wir sind sicher, daß Leonard Bernstein mit dieser überarbeiteten Klavierauszug zufrieden wäre, und hoffen, daß sie seiner Musik auf viele Jahre gute Dienste leistet.

Seann Alderking und Charlie Harmon
1999

Note du rédacteur

Lorsqu'en 1984 Leonard Bernstein conduisit *West Side Story* durant son enregistrement pour Deutsche Grammophon, il profita de l'occasion pour passer en revue la partition non seulement du point de vue d'un chef d'orchestre, mais aussi de celui d'un compositeur. Il fit plusieurs révisions, en précisant que celles-ci devraient figurer dans la version imprimée de la partition. On démarra immédiatement la préparation de la partition complète, mais le décès de M. Bernstein en 1990 l'interrompit. La partition complète fut imprimée par Boosey & Hawkes en 1994 et toutes les révisions de M. Bernstein furent incorporées dans cette édition.

Il est maintenant temps de publier une partition chant et piano pour y faire pendant. Nous avons donc profité de cette occasion pour revoir plusieurs éléments de la partition. Tout d'abord, il y a maintenant un comptage des mesures, avec des numéros de mesure dans des cases de répétition correspondant à ceux de la partition complète. Le nom de chaque personnage apparaît maintenant dans la marge de gauche, à coté de la musique qu'il chante. Des indications de rentrée des instruments sont fournies à travers toute la partition, de sorte que cette partition chant et piano peut être tout aussi bien considérée comme une partition piano orchestre. Les pages préliminaires ont été développées pour inclure l'instrumentation, des renseignements sur la concession de licence, la durée de l'œuvre et des renseignements sur l'enregistrement de Deutsche Grammophon.

Bien que M. Bernstein ait fait clairement connaître ses désirs en ce qui concerne « l'Ouverture », ne voulant pas qu'elle figure au début de la partition complète, nous en avons inclus ici une version abrégée pour piano sous forme d'annexe. Une seconde annexe comporte des renseignements sur la distribution et le générique de la version filmée de *West Side Story*. Veuillez noter que cette partition chant et piano révisée ne comprend aucune des modifications musicales du film ; cette partition présente cette œuvre comme originellement prévu pour la scène par les auteurs.

Du point de vue musical, cette partition chant et piano révisée reflète bien plus exactement ce qu'on trouve dans l'orchestration. Par exemple, dans la partition originale chant et piano, la main gauche, aux mesures 72 à 79 du « Mambo » jouait à contretemps en faisant beaucoup de bruit, mais ce n'était pas du tout ce que jouait l'orchestre. Ce passage a maintenant été modifié par mesure d'exactitude et pour pouvoir se jouer au piano. Au début du « Quintette », la main droite joue maintenant des octaves différentes conformément aux octaves que jouent les diverses sections de l'orchestre. Ailleurs, le début du numéro 13 (le ballet du second acte) avait été écrit sur trois portées ; ce passage est plus facile à lire sur deux portées dans la partition révisée, tout en conservant néanmoins toutes les notes.

Dans chaque cas, la musique semble maintenant plus accessible. Les lignes de chant sont plus faciles à lire avec des traits sur des groupes de notes de moins d'une noire. Dans la partition abrégée pour piano, la musique de danse terriblement difficile le reste toujours, mais on trouve maintenant des notes repères indiquant ce que vous pouvez omettre si la musique dépasse vos compétences techniques. De nombreux passages sont désormais mieux répartis entre les deux mains.

Nous désirons remercier Tom Hooper de l'aide experte qu'il nous a apportée pour introduire une grande partie de cette nouvelle édition dans des fichiers informatiques. Nos remerciements également à Holly Mentzer de Boosey & Hawkes, Inc. et à Rick Sanford.

Nous sommes certains que cette partition révisée aurait été bien accueillie par M. Bernstein et nous espérons qu'elle servira bien sa musique pendant de nombreuses années.

Seann Alderking et Charlie Harmon
1999

Characters and Vocal Ranges

Maria (Soprano)

Tony (Tenor)

Anita (Mezzo-soprano)

Riff (Baritone)

Rosalia

Francisca

Consuelo

Action

Baby John

Big Deal

A-rab

Snowboy

Diesel

Bernardo

A Girl

Chorus: Jets, Sharks, Their Girls

Speaking Roles:

Krupke
Schrank
Glad Hand
Offstage Voice of Maria's Mother
Offstage Voice of Maria's Father
Doc

Original Broadway Production Credits and Cast List

Robert E. Griffith and Harold S. Prince, by arrangement with Roger L. Stevens, first presented *West Side Story* on 26 September 1957, at the Winter Garden, New York City, with the following credits and cast:

WEST SIDE STORY

Based on a conception of Jerome Robbins

Book by Arthur Laurents
Music by Leonard Bernstein
Lyrics by Stephen Sondheim

Entire Production Directed and Choreographed by Jerome Robbins

Orchestration by Leonard Bernstein with Sid Ramin and Irwin Kostal
Musical Direction by Max Goberman
Scenic Production by Oliver Smith
Costumes Designed by Irene Sharaff
Lighting by Jean Rosenthal
Co-Choreographer: Peter Gennaro
Production Asscociate: Sylvia Drulie

THE JETS

Riff (The Leader)	Mickey Calin
Tony (His Friend)	Larry Kert
Action	Eddie Roll
A-rab	Tony Mordente
Baby John	David Winters
Snowboy	Grover Dale
Big Deal	Martin Charnin
Diesel	Hank Brunjes
Gee-Tar	Tommy Abbott
Mouthpiece	Frank Green
Tiger	Lowell Harris

THE SHARKS

Bernardo (The Leader)	Ken Le Roy
Maria (His Sister)	Carol Lawrence
Anita (His Girl)	Chita Rivera
Chino (His Friend)	Jamie Sanchez
Pepe	George Marcy
Indio	Noel Schwartz
Luis	Al De Sio
Anxious	Gene Gavin
Nibbles	Ronnie Lee
Juano	Jay Norman
Toro	Erne Castaldo
Moose	Jack Murray

THEIR GIRLS

Graziella	Wilma Curley
Velma	Carole D'Andrea
Minnie	Nanette Rosen
Clarice	Marilyn D'Honau
Pauline	Julie Oser
Anybodys	Lee Becker

THEIR GIRLS

Rosalia	Marilyn Cooper
Consuelo	Reri Grist
Teresita	Carmen Guiterrez
Francisca	Elizabeth Taylor
Estella	Lynn Ross
Margarita	Liane Plane

THE ADULTS

Doc	Art Smith
Schrank	Arch Johnson
Krupke	William Bramley
Glad Hand	John Harkins

Tony awards
Choreographer: Jerome Robbins
Scenic Designer: Oliver Smith

The original Broadway cast recording was first released on CBS OL 5320 (LP),
re-released on Columbia CK 64419 (CD) and Sony Classical SK 60724 (CD).

Leonard Bernstein Recording

West Side Story was recorded for Deutsche Grammophon (Hanno Rinke, executive producer; John McClure, recording producer) on 4, 5, 6, 7 September 1984, at the RCA Studios (110 West 44 Street), Studio A , New York City, and was released with the following credits and cast:

WEST SIDE STORY
Based on a conception of Jerome Robbins

Book by Arthur Laurents
Music by Leonard Bernstein
Lyrics by Stephen Sondheim

Entire Original Production Directed and Choreographed by Jerome Robbins

Orchestrations by Leonard Bernstein with Sid Ramin and Irwin Kostal

Musical Preparation and Rehearsal Conductor: David Stahl
Chorus Contractor: Adrienne Albert
Orchestra's Contracting Personnel Manager: Samuel Levitan
Rehearsal Pianist and Coach: Jim Stenborg
Dialect Coaching: Nico Castel

Coordination: Alison Ames, Claudia Hamann
Recording Engineer: Karl-August Naegler
Editing: Jobst Eberhardt, Wolf-Dieter Karwatky

Orchestra and Chorus
Conducted by Leonard Bernstein

Maria ....Kiri Te Kanawa
Tony...Carreras
Anita..Tatiana Troyanos
Riff ....Kurt Ollmann

and Marilyn Horne singing "Somewhere"

Rosalia..Louise Edeiken
Francisca ....Angelina Reaux
Consuelo...Stella Zambalis
Action..David Livingston
Diesel..Marty Nelson
Baby John ....Stephen Bogardus
A-rab...Peter Thom
Snowboy...Todd Lester
Bernardo ....Richard Harrell

Dialogue: Nina Bernstein (Maria), Alexander Bernstein (Tony)

LP: 415 253-1
CD: 415 253-2

•   •   •

Leonard Bernstein Conducts West Side Story, The Making of the Recording
(Humphrey Burton and Thomas P Skinner, Producers; Christopher Swann, director)
is a video presentation of the recording sessions.

Available from Deutsche Grammophon on
video cassette 072 206-3 and laserdisc 072 206-1

INSTRUMENTATION

Reed I: Piccolo, Flute, Alto Saxophone, Clarinet in B♭, Bass Clarinet
Reed II: Clarinet in E♭, Clarinet in B♭, Bass Clarinet
Reed III: Piccolo, Flute, Oboe, English Horn, Tenor Saxophone,
            Baritone Saxophone, Clarinet in B♭, Bass Clarinet
Reed IV: Piccolo, Flute, Soprano Saxophone, Bass Saxophone,
            Clarinet in B♭, Bass Clarinet
Reed V: Bassoon

2 Horns in F
3 Trumpets in B♭ (2nd doubling Trumpet in D)
2 Trombones
Timpani
Percussion (four players)*
Piano/Celesta
Electric Guitar/Spanish Guitar/Mandolin
Violin I–VII
Cello I–IV
Contrabass

*Traps, Vibraphone, 4 Pitched Drums, Guiro, Xylophone, 3 Bongos, 3 Cowbells, Conga, Timbales,
Snare Drum, Police Whistle, Gourd, 2 Suspended Cymbals, Castanets, Maracas, Finger Cymbals,
Tambourines, Small Maracas, Glockenspiel, Woodblock, Claves, Triangle,
Temple Blocks, Chimes, Tam-tam, Ratchet, Slide Whistle

Duration
Act I: 90 minutes
Act II: 45 minutes

*For first class, stock and amateur productions worldwide,
performancematerials are available in full or reduced orchestrations from Music Theatre International.*

*For concert suites and performances of individual numbers worldwide,
performance materials are available from Boosey & Hawkes.*

Also available from Boosey & Hawkes:

Two concert suites of selections from West Side Story, *for voices and orchestra;
Symphonic Dances from West Side Story;
Overture to West Side Story*

To Felicia, with love

WEST SIDE STORY
ACT ONE
1. Prologue

Instrumental

Lyrics by
Stephen Sondheim

Music by
Leonard Bernstein

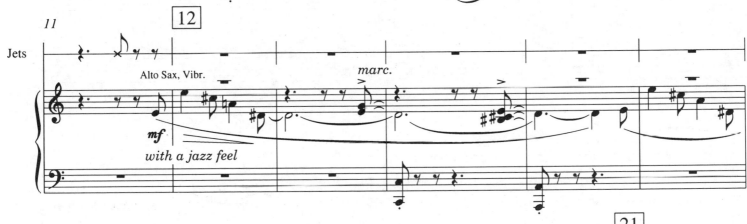

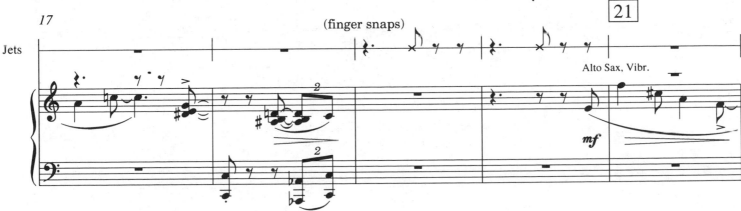

Slightly Faster

4

73 · Hns., Tpts. II & III, Tbns., El. Gtr., Pno., Vlns.

76

Picc., Cls., Tpt. I *(8ba)*, El. Gtr.

ff Traps, Guiro

f

Tbns. *gliss.*

78

(Baby John and A–rab enter.)

ff

Bs. Sax, Bsn., El. Gtr., Pno., Vcs., Cb.

84

83 · 4 Pitched Drums

p

p

Vcs. & Cb. *gliss.*

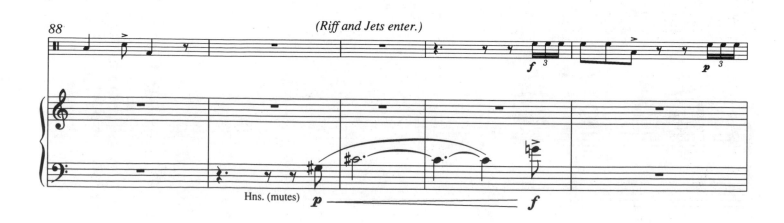

88

(Riff and Jets enter.)

f 3 · *p* 3

Hns. (mutes) *p* ———————— *f*

5

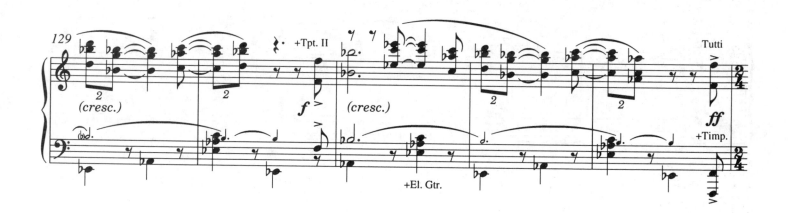

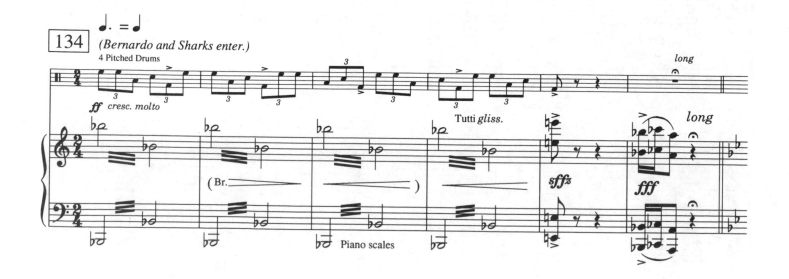

Più Mosso (scherzando e misterioso)

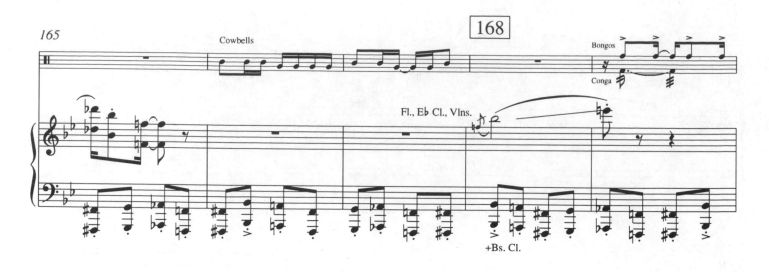

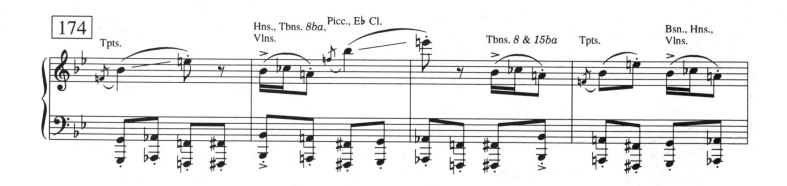

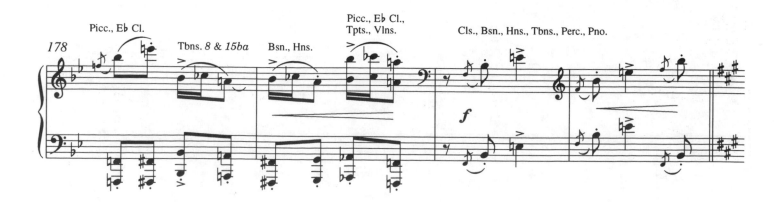

2. Jet Song

Riff and Jets

Cue: ACTION: Who needs Tony?

SNOWBOY
What about the day we clobbered the Emeralds?

A–RAB
Which we couldn't have done without Tony.

BABY JOHN
He saved my
ever–lovin' neck!

RIFF
Right! He's always come through for us and he will now.

* –de: bar 128 (p. 19); original Broadway Production. If cut is made, dialogue is as follows:

A–RAB: "Great, Daddy–O!" RIFF: "So everybody dress up sweet and sharp. Meet Tony and me at ten."

Applause Segue

2a. Jet Song Chase

Change of Scene
Instrumental

3. Something's Coming

Tony

Cue: RIFF: Maybe what you're waitin' for will be
twitchin' at the dance. (*He runs off.*)

It's __ on - ly just __ out of reach, __

dim. sempre

181

Down the block, __ on a beach, __ May - be to - night ..._____

+Tpts. (sust.)

sempre dim.   −Vlns.

dim.   ┌ - - - - - - - *Safety* - - - - - - ┐
(fade out)

(dim.)   *fade out*

Applause Segue

3a. Something's Coming Chase

Change of Scene
Instrumental

4. The Dance at the Gym

Blues
Instrumental

Cue: MARIA: Because tonight is the real beginning
of my life as a young lady of America!

(Bernardo enters with Maria, Anita and Chino. As the Jets see them they drop out of the dance one by one and withdraw to one side of the hall. The Sharks draw to their side.)

(Repeat, if necessary, and cut off as the two gangs move toward each other.)

4a. Promenade
Instrumental

Cue: GLAD HAND: All right: here we go!

4b. Mambo
Instrumental

46

(Tony and Maria see each other.)

ALL JETS & SHARKS

Go, Mam - bo! Go, Mam - bo! Go, Mam -

bo!

All

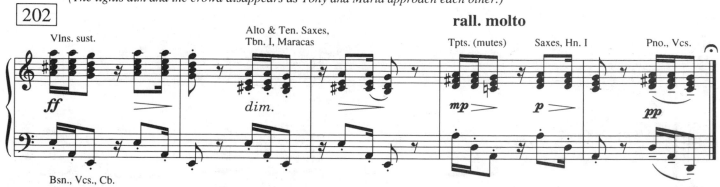

(The lights dim and the crowd disappears as Tony and Maria approach each other.)

rall. molto

Segue

4c. Cha – Cha

Instrumental

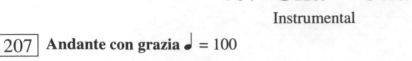

El. Gtr., Fngr. Cyms.

Piano

Cl., Bsn., Vcs., Cb. (pizz.)

211

3 Fls., Bongos, Tamb.,
Pno., Vlns. (pizz.)

210

light and dry

214   KIDS   (finger snaps)

217

+Maracas

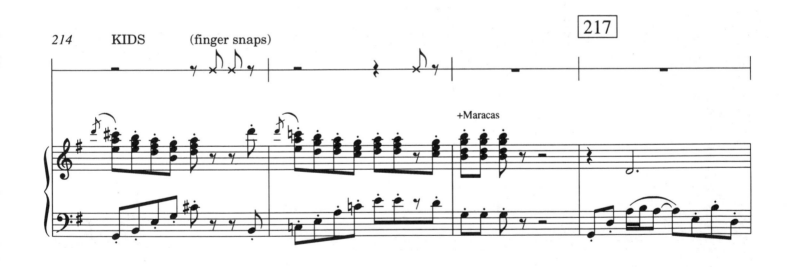

218

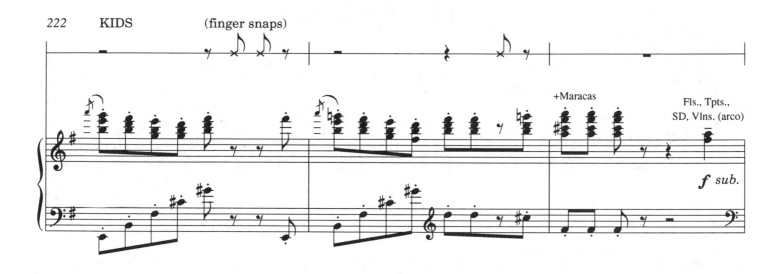

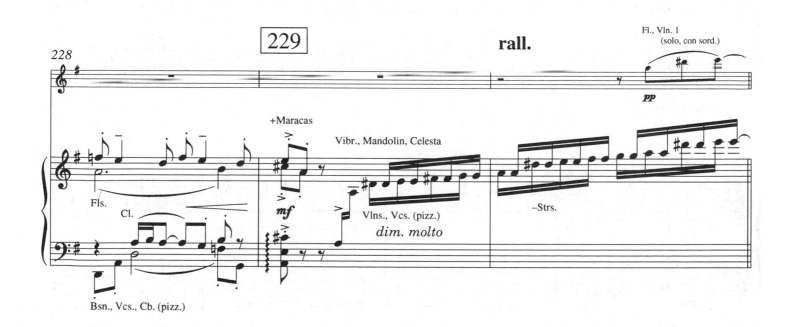

4d. Meeting Scene

Underscore

Cue: TONY:
You're not thinking
I'm someone else?

MARIA
I know you are not.

TONY
Or that we've met before?

MARIA
I know we have not.

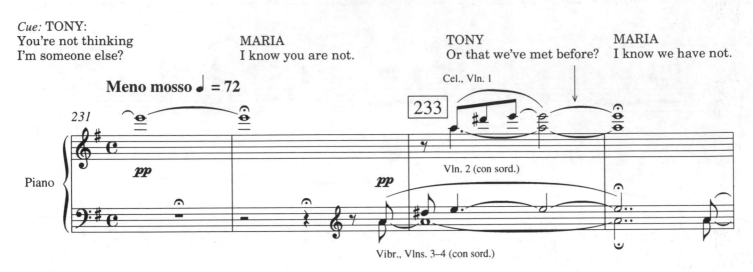

TONY
I felt,
I knew …
But this is …

MARIA
My hands
are so cold.

*(He takes them
in his.)*

Yours, too.

*(He moves her
hands to his face.)*

So warm.

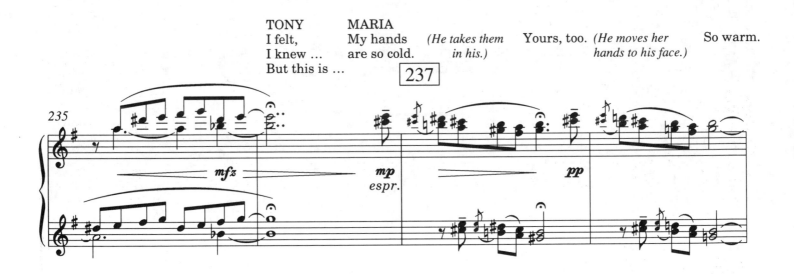

TONY
Yours, too.

MARIA
But of course.
They are the same.

TONY
It's so much
to believe.

You're not
joking me?

MARIA
I have not yet learned
to joke that way.
I think now I never will

52

4e. Jump
Underscore

Lo stesso tempo, fast, light, dry

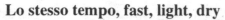

Repeat, if necessary, and fade at Cue: RIFF:
Let's get the chicks and kick it.

5. Maria

Tony

Cue: DIESEL: We'll see him at Doc's.

TONY: Maria …

Slowly and freely

TONY

The most beau - ti - ful sound I ev - er heard: Ma -

cresc.

ri - a, Ma - ri - a, Ma - ri - a, Ma - ri - a…

All the beau - ti - ful sounds of the world in a sin - gle word: Ma -

* Original Broadway production: The repeated "Marias" were sung by off-stage voices.

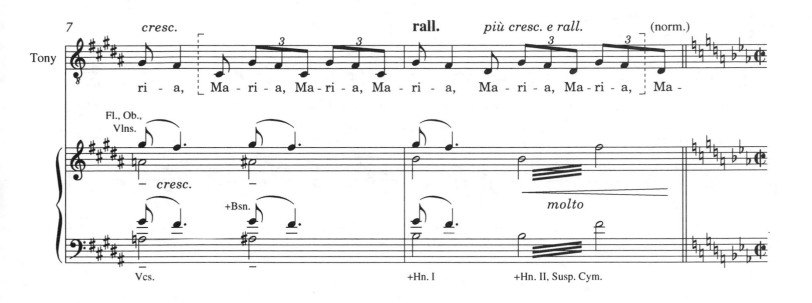

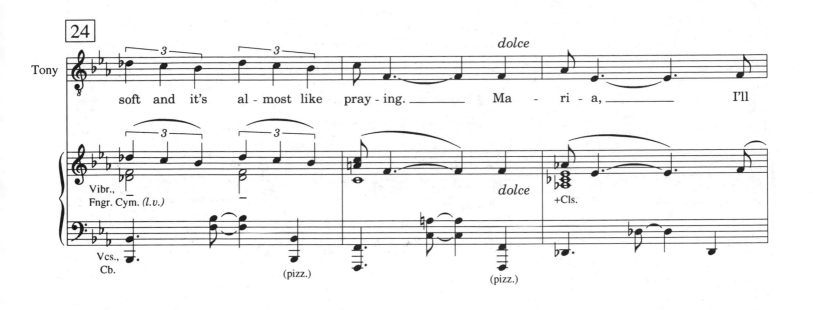

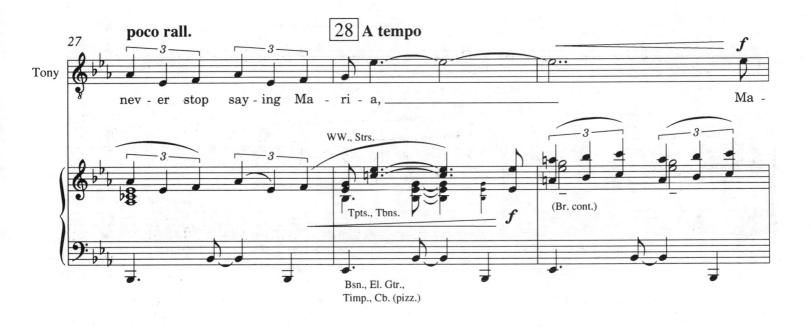

Applause Segue

6. Balcony Scene

Maria and Tony

7. America

Anita, Rosalia and Girls

Cue: ROSALIA: That's a very pretty name: Etcetera.

Moderato, Tempo di "Seis"

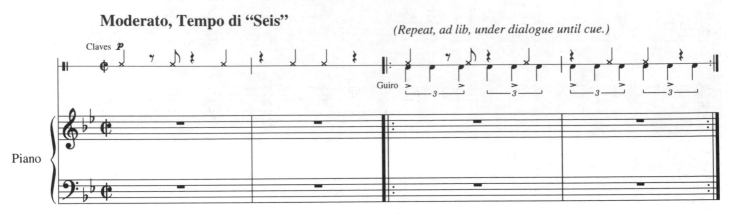

ROSALIA: Just for a successful visit.

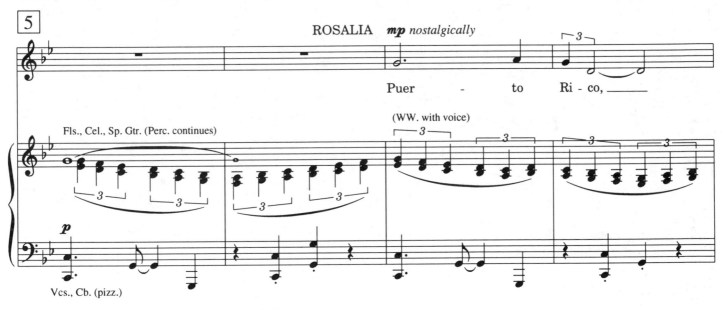

* Optional

(The girls whistle and dance around Rosalia.)

* Optional

Applause Segue

7a. America to Drugstore

Change of Scene
Instrumental

Tempo di Huapango (fast)

(Fade when lights come up)

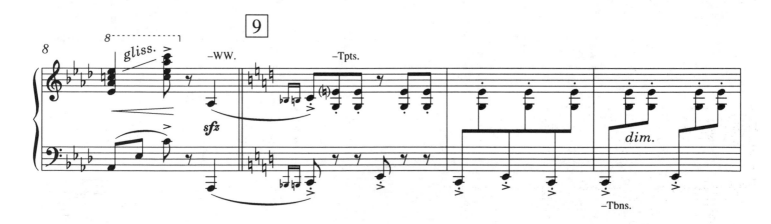

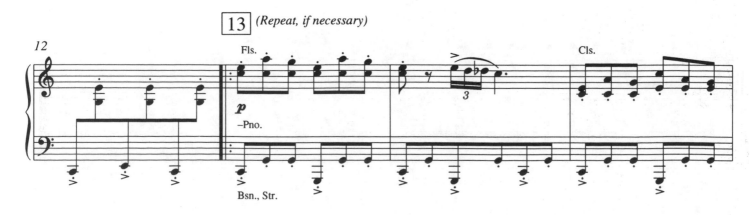

90

8. Cool

Riff and Jets

31

Riff

Go, man, go, — But not like a yo-yo school-boy._____ Just___ play it

dim. molto

Vibr., El. Gtr.
Pno., Bs. Cl.

Fl., Vibr., El. Gtr.,
Pno.

mp
+Br. (cup mutes)

dim. molto

35
pp sub.

37

Riff

cool, boy,_____ Real _____ cool!_____

pp

Vcs., Cb. (pizz.)

+Bsn., Pno.

39

Poco più mosso

Vibr., El. Gtr.
Pno.

Traps Hi-hat

Pno., Cb.

43 [FUGUE]

Tpt. I (cup mute)

+Tpts. II & III (open)

Vibr., El. Gtr.

pp cresc.
(Traps continue)

Traps HH

molto

sfz

(Traps cont.)

pp

Tpt. I
–Pno.

SD rim shot

–Cb.

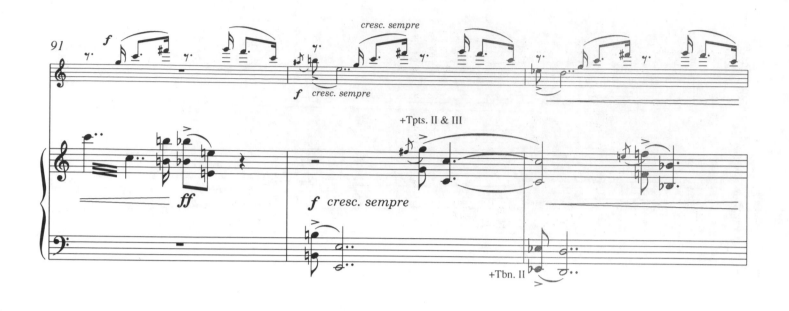

cool,   boy, _____   Real _____ cool! _____

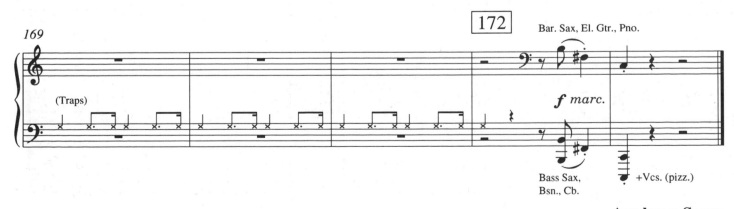

Applause Segue

8a. Cool Chase

Continuation of Scene
Instrumental

(They resume dancing.)

Lo stesso tempo

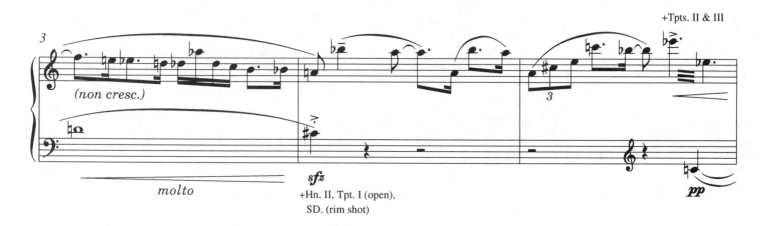

8b. Under Dialogue
and Change of Scene
Underscore and Instrumental

Cue: TONY: Forget him. From here on in, everything goes my way.   DOC: You think it'll really be a

fair fight?   TONY: Yeah.   DOC: What have you been takin' tonight?   TONY: A trip to the moon. And

I'll tell you a secret. It isn't a man that's up there, Doc. It's a girl, a lady. *(opens the door) Buenas noches,*

señor.   DOC: *Buenas noches*?! So that's why you made it a fair fight. Tony, things aren't tough enough?

TONY: Tough? Doc, I'm in love!   DOC: How do you know?   TONY: Because there isn't any other way

104

I could feel.   DOC: And you're not frightened?   TONY: Why should I be? *(Exits.)*

DOC: Why? I'm frightened enough for both of you.

9. Under Dialogue

Underscore

TONY
You go home and dress up.   Then tonight I will come by for you.

MARIA
You cannot come by. My mama …

TONY
Then I will take
you to my house—

MARIA
(shaking her head)
Your mama …

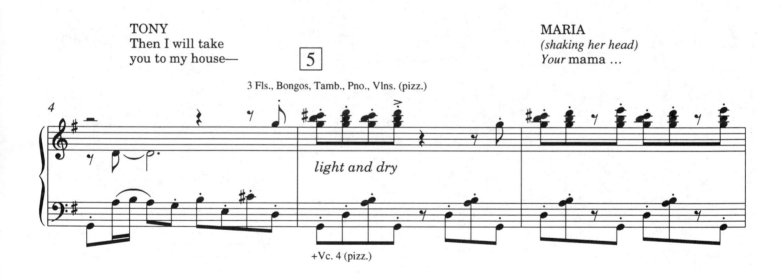

TONY
(Pulling up a female dummy.)
She will come running from the kitchen to welcome you.

She lives in the
kitchen.

MARIA Dressed so elegant?

TONY I told her you
were coming.

TONY
She will look at your face
and try not to smile.
And she will say:

Skinny — but pretty.

MARIA
She is plump, no doubt.

TONY
(Holding the waist
of dummy's dress.)
Fat!

MARIA
(Arranging another female dummy.)
I take after my mama; delicate boned. (He kisses her.)

MARIA
Not in front
of Mama!

(She goes to a male dummy.)
Oh, I would like to see Papa in this!
(He turns the "mama" dummy around.)

MARIA
Mama will make him ask
about your prospects,   if you go to church.   But Papa —   Papa *might* like you.

TONY
(kneeling to the "father" dummy.)
May I have your daughter's hand?

MARIA
He says yes.

TONY
Gracias!

MARIA
And your mama?

TONY
I'm afraid to ask her.

MARIA
Tell her she's not getting a daughter; she's getting rid of a son!

TONY
She says yes.

MARIA
She has good taste.

TONY
(He continues to arrange the dummies.)
Maid of honor!

MARIA
That color is bad for Anita.

MARIA
(She puts on a wedding veil.)

TONY
Best man!

MARIA
That is my Papa!

TONY
Sorry, Papa. Here we go, Riff: womb to tomb!

(He takes hat off dummy.)

MARIA
Now you see, Anita, I told you there was nothing to worry about.

TONY
Mama's crying already.

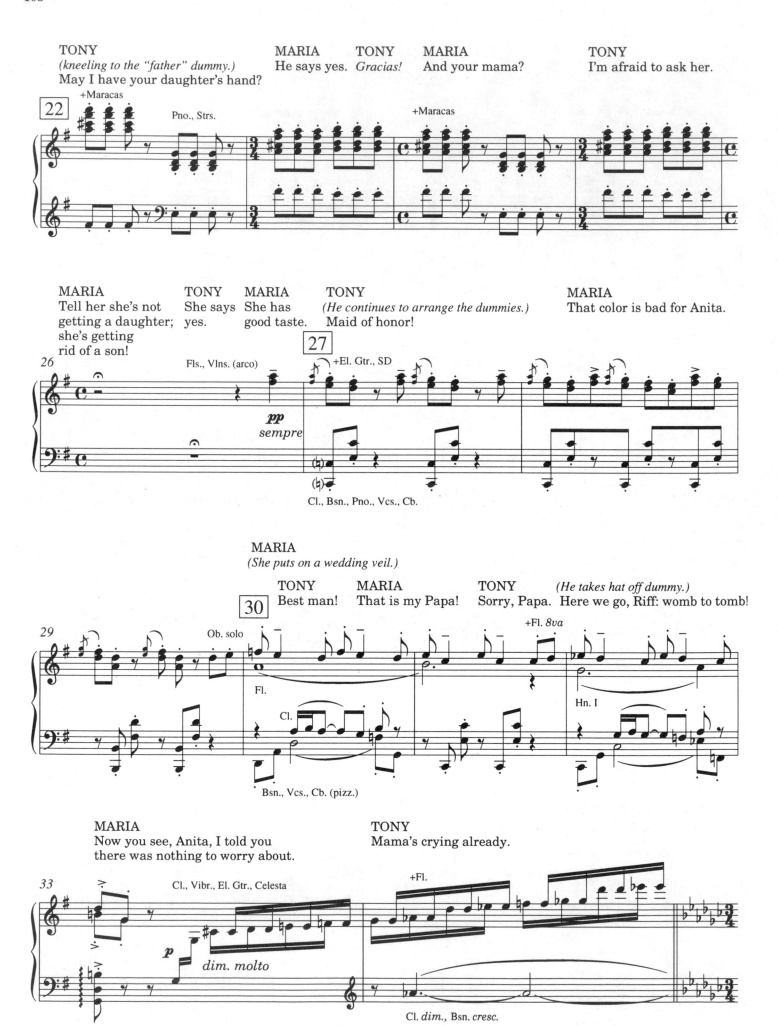

9a. One Hand, One Heart
(Marriage Scene)

Tony and Maria

114

10. Tonight

Ensemble
Maria, Tony, Anita, Riff, Bernardo*
Sharks and Jets

* If the scene is staged with more than the designated five people, the members of the gangs may sing with their respective leaders (except in bars 103 - 125).

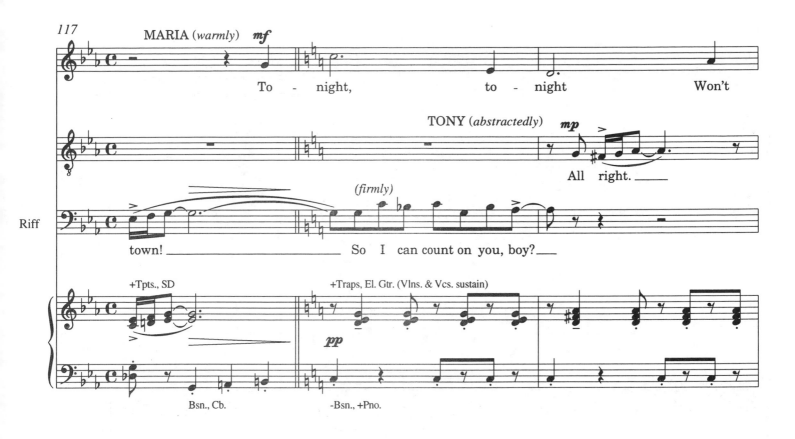

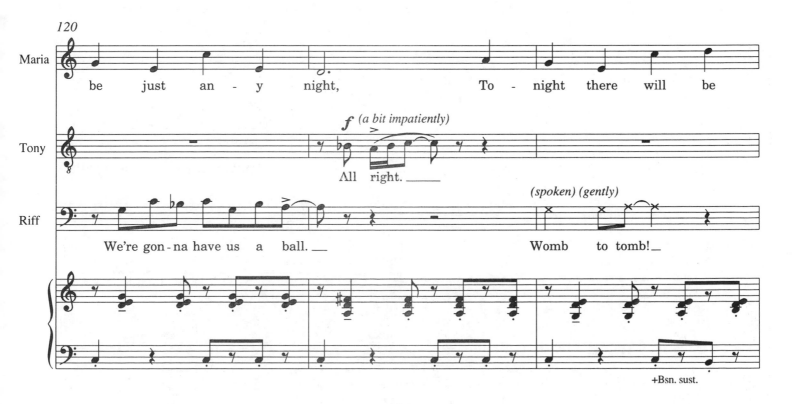

* The part of Anita may be augmented by voices in the wings from here to the end.

* The part of Maria may be augmented by voices in the wings from here to the end.

11. The Rumble

Instrumental

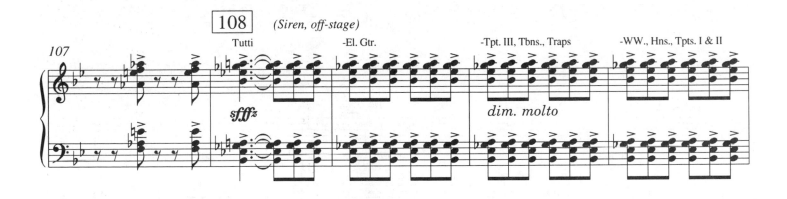

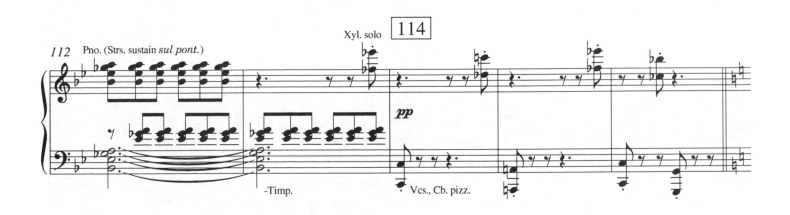

*Hold fermata until curtain is down.

END of ACT ONE

ACT TWO
12. I Feel Pretty

Maria, Francisca, Rosalia, Consuelo

Francisca: too much to eat

Rosalia: Or may - be it's fleas.

244 | unis.

Francisca / Rosalia / Consuelo: Keep a - way from her, Send for Chi - no!

248

Francisca / Rosalia / Consuelo: This is not the Ma - ri - a a we know!

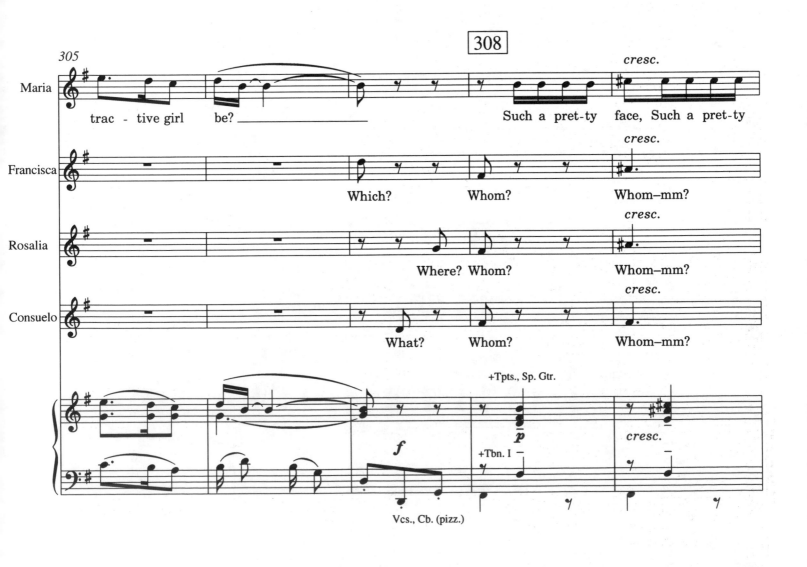

13. Under Dialogue

Underscore, Tony

Cue: MARIA: Killer, killer, killer ...

Allegro agitato (♩ = 108+)

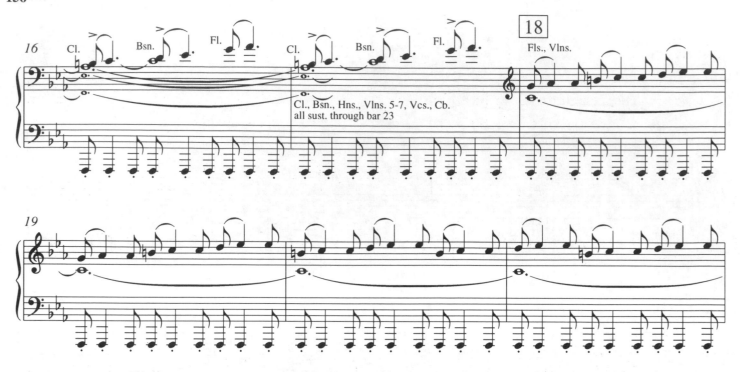

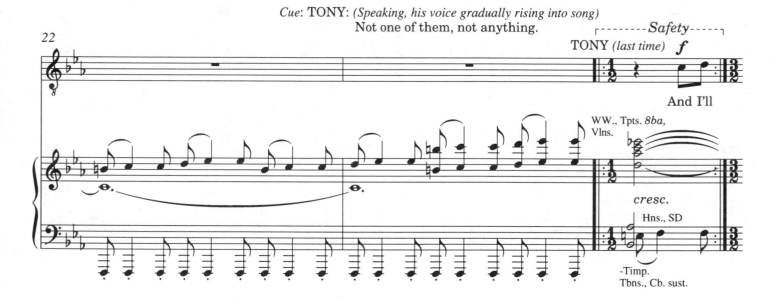

13a. Ballet Sequence

Tony and Maria

(Ballet Sequence continued)

13b. Transition to Scherzo

Instrumental

(Ballet Sequence continued)

13c. Scherzo

Instrumental

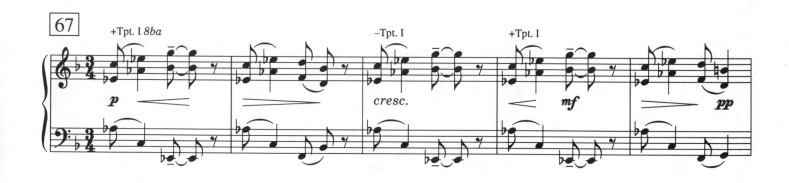

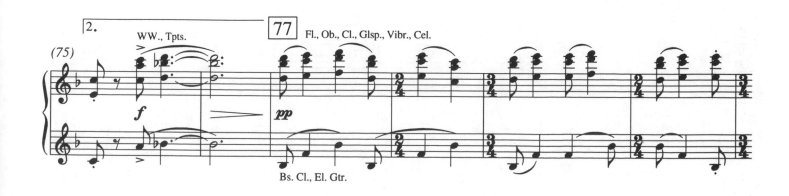

(Ballet Sequence continued)

13d. Somewhere

A Girl

Segue

(Ballet Sequence continued)

13e. Procession and Nightmare

Entire Company, Instrumental, Maria and Tony

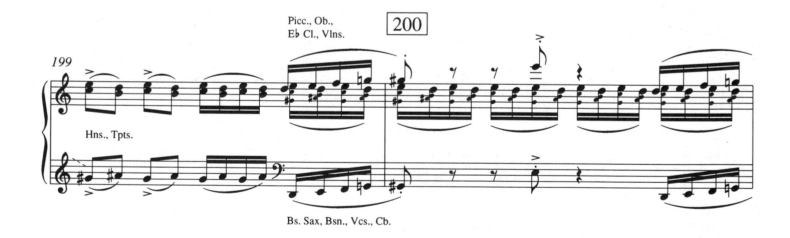

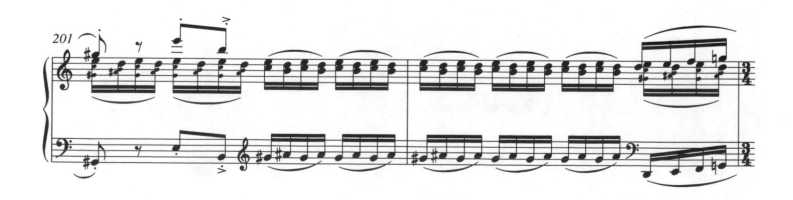

14. Gee, Officer Krupke

Jets

Cue: ACTION: We're cruddy juvenile delinquents.
So that's what we give 'em.

Fast, vaudeville style

Cue: SNOWBOY: Just tell it to the Judge.

El. Gtr., Traps,
Pno., Strs.

101

Cue: DIESEL: So take him to a headshrinker.

105 **106** Picc., Fl., Vlns.

Safety

p sub.

f

Bsn., Hns., Tbns.

Tpts.

ACTION (to A-RAB) *(last time)* **111**

109 Safety

My   fa - ther is a bas - tard,   My

Cls., Hns.

p sub.

Traps, El. Gtr., Pno., Vlns., Cb. (Vcs. sust.)

113

Action   ma's an S. O. B.   My grand-pa's al - ways plas - tered,   My

131

a-rab
boy don't need a doc - tor, just a good hon - est job. ____ So -

Bsn.

Tbns.

135

A-rab
ci - e - ty's played ____ him a ter - ri - ble trick, ____

cresc.

cresc.

+Br.

139

ACTION *ff*
I am sick! We are

A-rab
And so - cio - lo - gic - 'ly he's sick!

JETS *ff*
We are

Cls., Strs.

f

p

152

El. Gtr., Traps,
Pno., Strs.

Cue: A-RAB: So take him to a social worker.

156

157

Picc., Fl., Vlns.

Bsn., Hns., Tbns.

160

ACTION (to BABY JOHN) *(last time)* 162

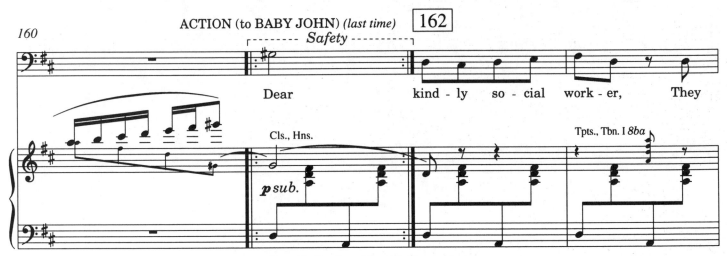

Dear kind-ly so-cial work-er, They

Cls., Hns.

Tpts., Tbn. I *8ba*

Traps, El. Gtr., Pno., Vlns., Cb. (Vcs. sust.)

164

Action

say go earn a buck. Like be a so-da jerk-er, Which

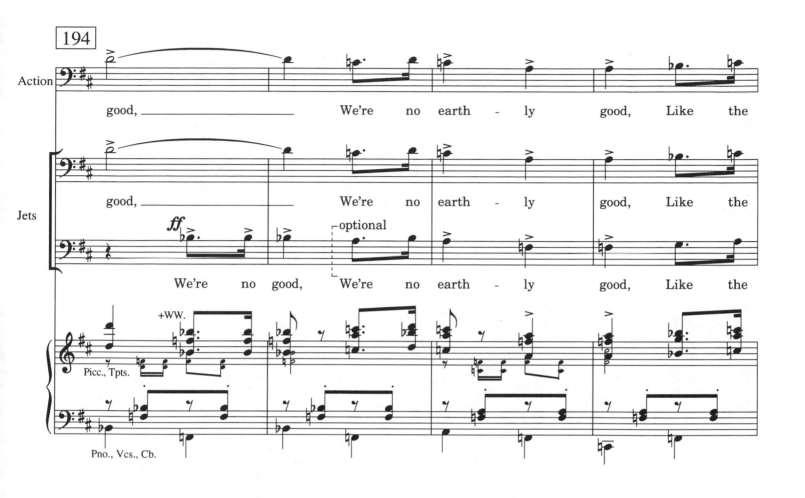

14a. Change of Scene

Instrumental

Cue: ANYBODYS: Thanks, Daddy-o.

15. A Boy Like That
and I Have A Love
Duet
Maria and Anita

Cue: ANITA: And you still don't know: Tony is one of them!

194

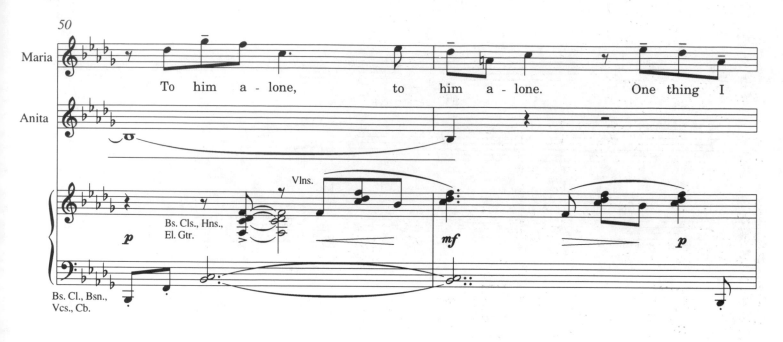

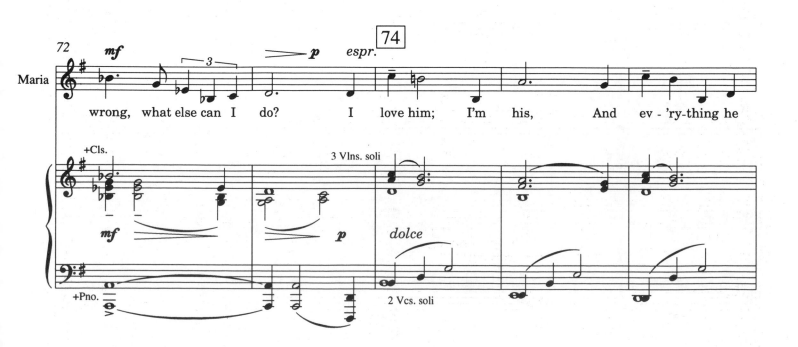

15a. Change of Scene

Instrumental

Tempo di prologue

(Cut off when Jets run into drugstore.)

16. Taunting Scene *

Underscore and Instrumental

(A coin is put in the Juke Box.)

* The Mambo section of this scene is pre-recorded and must seem to be coming from the Juke Box.

208

Cue: ACTION: Spic! Lyin' Spic!

17. Finale

Maria and Tony

Cue: TONY: Yes we can. We *will.*

Adagio

MARIA
mp

Hold my hand and we're half - way there. Hold my hand and I'll

TONY *mp cresc.*

Hold my hand and I'll

Piano

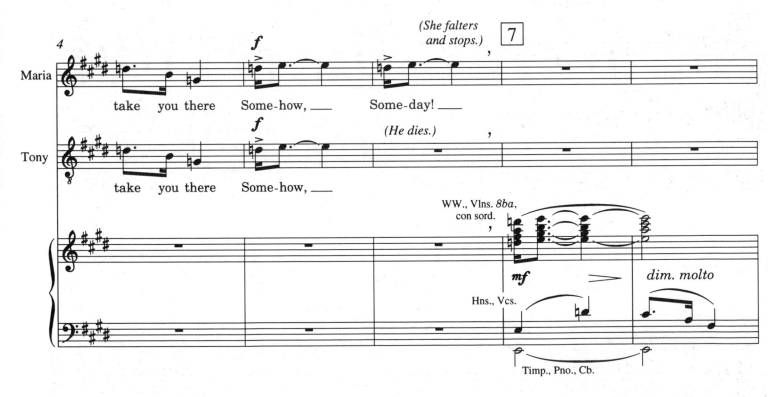

4

Maria

take you there Some-how, ___ Some-day! ___

(She falters and stops.) 7

Tony

take you there Some-how, ___

(He dies.)

WW., Vlns. *8ba,* con sord.

mf dim. molto

Hns., Vcs.

Timp., Pno., Cb.

MARIA: Stay back!
(Dialogue continues)

9

Vlns.

3

long

pp *ppp*

Vcs.

Cue: MARIA: *Te adoro, Anton.*

Meno mosso

SLOW CURTAIN

26 **Ancora meno mosso**

Appendix
Overture
Instrumental

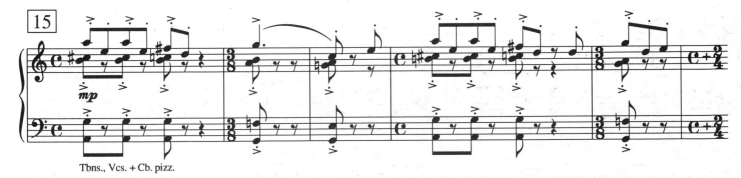

Mirisch Pictures, Inc., presented a Robert Wise production, filmed in association with Seven Arts Productions for United Artists release, of *West Side Story* on 18 October 1961, with the following credits and cast:

WEST SIDE STORY

Produced by Robert Wise
Directed by Robert Wise and Jerome Robbins
Screenplay by Ernest Lehman
Associate Producer: Saul Chaplin
Choreography by Jerome Robbins
Music by Leonard Bernstein
Lyrics by Stephen Sondheim
Based upon the stage play produced by Robert E. Griffith and Harold S. Prince
by arrangement with Robert L. Stevens
Book by Arthur Laurents

Play conceived, directed and choreographed by Jerome Robbins

Film production designed by Boris Leven
Music conducted by Johnny Green

Filmed in Panavision 70 Technicolor
In association with Seven Arts Productions, Inc.
Released through United Artists

Director of Photography: Daniel L Fapp, ASC
Costumes designed by Irene Sharaff
Assistant Director: Robert E Relyea
Dance Assistants: Tommy Abbott, Margaret Banks, Howard Jeffrey, Tony Mordente
Film Editor: Thomas Stanford
Music Editor: Richard Carruth
Photographic effects: Linwood Dunn, ASC, Film Effects of Hollywood
Orchestrations by Sid Ramin and Irwin Kostal
Sound by Murray Spivack, Fred Lau and Vinton Vernon
Musical Assistant: Betty Walberg
Vocal Coach: Bobby Tucker
Production Manager: Allen K Wood
Titles and Visual Consultation by Saul Bass and Associates
Production Artist: M. Zuberano
Set Decorator: Victor Gangelin
Property: Sam Gordon
Sound Editor: Gilbert D. Marchant
Assistant Editor: Marshall M Borden
Script Supervisor: Stanley K Scheuer
Second Assistant Director: Jerome M Siegel
Make-up: Emile La Vigne, SMA
Hairdresser: Alice Monte, CHS
Wardrobe: Bert Henrikson
Casting: Stalmaster-Lister Co.

THE CAST

Maria	Natalie Wood
Tony	Richard Beymer
Riff	Russ Tamblyn
Anita	Rita Moreno
Bernardo	George Chakiris

THE JETS

Ice	Tucker Smith
Action	Tony Mordente
A-rab	David Winters
Baby John	Eliot Feld
Snowboy	Bert Michaels
Tiger	David Bean
Joyboy	Robert Banas
Big Deal	Scooter Teague
Mouthpiece	Harvey Hohnecker
Gee-Tar	Tommy Abbott

THE SHARKS

Chino	Jose De Vega
Pepe	Jay Norman
Indio	Gus Trikonis
Juano	Eddie Verso
Loco	Jaime Rogers
Rocco	Larry Roquemore
Luis	Robert Thompson
Toro	Nick Covacevich
Del Campo	Rudy Del Campo
Chile	Andre Tayir

THEIR GIRLS

Anybodys	Sue Oakes
Graziella	Gina Trikonis
Velma	Carole D'Andrea

THEIR GIRLS

Consuelo	Yvonne Othon
Rosalia	Suzie Kaye
Francisca	Joanne Miya

THE ADULTS

Lieutenant Schrank	Simon Oakland
Officer Krupke	William Bramley
Doc	Ned Glass
Glad Hand	John Astin
Madam Lucia	Penny Santon

Marni Nixon sang the role of Maria.
Jim Bryant sang the role of Tony.
Portions of the role of Anita were sung by
Marni Nixon and Betty Wand.

Academy Awards (Oscars®) from the Academy of Motion Picture Arts and Sciences:
Best Picture, Directors, Supporting Actor (George Chakiris), Supporting Actress (Rita Moreno),
Color Cinematography, Color Art Direction, Sound (Todd-AO Sound Department, Samuel Goldwyn
Sound Department), Scoring of a Musical Picture, Editing, Color Costume Design.
Also nominated for Best Adapted Screenplay.

The soundtrack recording of music from the film was originally released on CBS OL 5670 LP,
re-released on SONY Masterworks CD SK48211.

Videocassette: MGM VHS M205296
DVD: MGM/UA 906733